Dress *for* Success

An Instant Diary for Christian Women

MARIANNE WOOD

WESTBOW
PRESS®
A DIVISION OF THOMAS NELSON
& ZONDERVAN

THE HOLY BIBLE, NEW INTERNATIONAL VERSION®,
NIV® Copyright © 1973, 1978, 1984, 2011 by Biblica, Inc.®
Used by permission. All rights reserved worldwide.

This book is a work of non-fiction. Unless otherwise noted, the author
and the publisher make no explicit guarantees as to the accuracy of
the information contained in this book and in some cases, names of
people and places have been altered to protect their privacy.

WestBow Press books may be ordered through booksellers or by contacting:

WestBow Press
A Division of Thomas Nelson & Zondervan
1663 Liberty Drive
Bloomington, IN 47403
www.westbowpress.com
1 (866) 928-1240

Because of the dynamic nature of the Internet, any web addresses or
links contained in this book may have changed since publication and
may no longer be valid. The views expressed in this work are solely those
of the author and do not necessarily reflect the views of the publisher,
and the publisher hereby disclaims any responsibility for them.

Any people depicted in stock imagery provided by Thinkstock are models,
and such images are being used for illustrative purposes only.
Certain stock imagery © Thinkstock.

ISBN: 978-1-5127-6430-7 (sc)
ISBN: 978-1-5127-6432-1 (hc)
ISBN: 978-1-5127-6431-4 (e)

Library of Congress Control Number: 2016919098

Print information available on the last page.

WestBow Press rev. date: 11/21/2016

For Megan, Molly, Jenny, and Sarah

My Journey and Testimony

One year my pastor's wife asked me to lead a class for young women. To get us started, she offered me her support, a teaching tool, and her first born daughter—as a student. That beginning led to this book. It meets my long-held need to write down some of the many, many helpful things I've have discovered in my personal journey with Christ.

That journey includes my conversion to Christianity at age twelve while singing "I Surrender All" at Camp Butman near my home in Abilene, Texas. Invited to a youth retreat by good friend and neighbor, Fredda Bedford (now Rosenbaum), I'm sure her family had laid groundwork through prayer before I ever got to the camp. I heard God's invitation loud and clear while singing that wonderful hymn.

While raised to know God by my dad and by people in my church, I had yet to comprehend the gospel of Jesus Christ until this experience.

Faithful fourth-grade Sunday school teachers, Bob and Margaret McCathren, had also put truth in my path. They ministered to me as a teen, and for thirty years we attended the same Bible church. What a joy it was to worship with them!

My advanced academic journey began in Columbia, Missouri at a small liberal arts college called Stephens. When my interior design program was discontinued, I transferred to the University of Texas at Arlington in route to Texas Tech University in Lubbock where I earned a BFA in interior design. At Tech I attended an activity called "Friday Night Tape Class (FNTC)." University students filled the living room of a fraternity house on Friday nights to listen to a cassette tape. This activity greatly contrasted with the rounds of fraternity parties I had experienced in Columbia. Thankfully, my Christian roommate at Stephens had helped me stay grounded during that phase. I am grateful for the opportunity to have seen the world that is now familiarly depicted on television (not much seems to have changed), but at FNTC, I finally found home.

These tape class students shared my commitment to Christ and enjoyed being together for class and for ski trips. (Lubbock is close enough to ski areas that it is not unusual for students to work ski patrol on the weekends.) It was understood that accommodations on ski trips were "women in one area, men in another." And when we met for class, we met in a well-lit room. The teaching we heard by Dr. S. Lewis Johnson from Believer's Chapel in Dallas easily gripped my attention and challenged me. It was all so refreshing!

After graduation I found work and a great church in Longview, Texas that took me further in my walk and gave me my first taste of teaching. Oakland Heights Baptist Church had a thriving college and career class that became so close one year that we collectively produced a Christmas card. We called ourselves "the Burger family," and I illustrated our card. There, I attended an Evangelism Explosion class, and they let me teach ninth grade girls—after I got baptized the Baptist way.

As a baby of a Presbyterian, I was duly sprinkled shortly after arrival. And after becoming a believer in Christ, I knew I needed to be baptized as a testimony to my new relationship. Years flew by, and it was not until a weekend scheduled at Pine Cove Camp near Tyler, Texas offered me the opportunity to make arrangements to get dunked in the camp pond. But there was a problem. A storm threatened the area the morning of my appointment. So the camp pastor poured the water over my head while I sat on the deck. Given to understand that the Jordan River occasionally got so low that some "Bible-times" people received the sacrament in the same way, I was satisfied.

But the Baptists were not. While my pastor at Oakland Heights agreed that I was "in" as far as he was concerned, rules were rules. I had to be dunked to qualify to teach ninth-grade girls in Baptist Sunday school. So I made a new appointment.

Since I had enjoyed the fact that ducks attended my last baptism at the pond, I told a friend I was sorry there could be none in the auditorium at OHBC. Imagine his wonder and mine when a white bird flew in during my baptism. Perhaps it was a sign. Perhaps not. But I'll never regret the result that came with this compliance. I got to teach ninth-grade girls, and consequently, I fell in love with teaching young women.

As I raised my own daughter and occasionally subbed for our teaching leader at Bible Study Fellowship, I anticipated the opportunity to share the steps in my journey with Christ. It is with great pleasure that I record for your growth, and occasionally your entertainment, some lessons and some questions to take you farther on your journey with Christ. The last segment, *Homiletics*, teaches the art of analyzing a Bible passage for personal or public enrichment. I thank BSF for sharing this skill with me.

Some Recommended Reading

Five Favorite Books of Faith outside the Bible

Talking with God by François Fénelon

Fenelon was a seventeenth-century priest in the court of King Louis XIV. He wrote about true prayer of the heart, how to use one's time wisely, the best kind of love, what to do when feelings fail us, and our union with God. In this short work you will find beautiful statements such as this: "...perfect prayer is only another name for love of God..."

Mere Christianity by C.S. Lewis

This book will blow you away. I put it up there with *To Kill a Mockingbird* as one of my top ten favorite books in any category. Lewis is brilliant in contending for the faith.

My Utmost for His Highest by Oswald Chambers

Oswald Chambers was my daily companion for about a decade as I read this devotional compiled by his widow, Gertrude. His "perfect delightful friendship" with our Lord has inspired me to find deeper fellowship.

In His Steps (What Would Jesus Do?) by Charles M. Sheldon

You thought the bracelets came first. Wrong. First published in 1896, this work of fiction describes a congregation that chooses to take its pastor's challenge to not do anything without first asking the title question. Their activities in undertaking the challenge drive the narrative.

The Pilgrim's Progress from This World to That Which Is to Come by John Bunyan

This Christian classic is a must-read. The pictures you will develop in your mind will stick with you in a helpful way. But if you prefer to see someone else's pictures, there is an illustrated version.

I also recommend the works of Philip Keller, Max Lucado, and Chuck Swindoll. Philip Keller's *A Shepherd Looks at Psalm 23* taught me the value of understanding the Scriptures better by getting close to the subject. What he taught me about sheep (and their likeness to people) still instructs. Max Lucado, similarly, never fails to paint a clear picture. His book, *The Great House of God,* is so graphic (in the good way) that I chose to draw the floor plan he suggests. Chuck Swindoll is electric in person, on the radio, and in print. *Living above the Level of Mediocrity* helped secure my commitment to a higher standard in work and in relationships. I remember reading that there are four major attractions in life: fame, fortune, power, and pleasure. All provide dangers if we don't have our hearts and minds in the right place. Bible studies by Audrey Wethererl Johnson, Kay Arthur and Beth Moore have had a huge impact on me also. Jane Pope, a former Bible Study Fellowship leader and a personal mentor, taught me the importance of looking at life through the "grid of God's word." This struck a special chord because my art training taught me about another grid known as "Alberti's Veil." Renaissance polymath Leon Battista Alberti described how an artist could get a correct view of a scene by observing it through a thin veil, or *velo.* The idea is that we can get a correct image of some object seen through such a veil or a window by tracing the outline of the object on the window glass. Albrecht Durer designed several such machines."

See the image here:

http://www.dartmouth.edu/~matc/math5.geometry/unit11/unit11.html

So if we can get better observations of the natural world from a grid, it made sense that we can also get a better picture of it from an overlay of the Bible. Thank you, Jane.

Today I am enjoying Sarah Young's devotional guide, *Jesus Calling: Enjoying Peace in His Presence.* It fits well with my current work which requires very heavy reading. Find what works for your season of life to keep you close to the source of life. I hope that this diary meets your need for that right now.

The Actual Introduction

The title, *Dress for Success*, has a double meaning for me. First, anticipating my first professional job, I purchased *Glamour Magazine's* book by that title. This practical how-to book from the 1970s helped me summon the courage to interview for my first job as an interior designer. A number of years later, when my job title became "Mom," I wrote my first book about dressing for success using the Bible's pictures for proper spiritual clothing found in Ephesians 6. It is my sincere hope that the contents of this version of dressing for success will be helpful to you as you meet both the natural and the spiritual worlds clothed with God's grace.

Acknowledgements

I wish to note here that the format for the book is inspired by (Philipp) *Keel's Simple Diary*. I discovered this fun tool for self-discovery in a favorite shop. On what amounted to a whim or possibly feminine intuition, I purchased three copies including two for gifts. After trying it out for a few days, I was hooked, and I put it away during the Christmas holidays while I worked on an early version of this book.

When I told my daughter, Laurie, what I was writing she dubbed it an "instant diary." Thanks, Laurie. I like the immediacy of that.

Conversations with Laurie and other close friends are at the heart of this book. Soon I realized that I'd have to write a special version for my Sunday school class. My students' names are on the first page. So not only is the book dedicated to them, but it was created for them, and I wish to thank them for their part of my inspiration. Their eagerness to learn what I had to share drove this work. If I seem to be smiling in my lesson prompts and questions, it is because I can see their faces in my mind.

There will be other acknowledgments throughout the diary. I did not learn these things in a vacuum cleaner.

Even though this work focuses on women, I must not fail to mention that one man is also at the heart of this book: my husband and true companion, Larry Wood. He is also a gifted editor. Thank you, Dear One.

Directions

The rest of the diary is in this simple format.

- Three Months
- Three Days a Week
- Three Graces (TBtG)–three each day

Fill in the month and year page. List any goals and objectives you have for that time period. Then turn to the next page and fill in the date.

Next, record three graces or thanksgivings noted with the shorthand: TBtG = "Thanks Be to God." I have found that thanking God daily for at least three things, often before my feet hit the floor in the morning, gets me in the right frame of mind for discovering God's purpose in the coming day.

Read the lessons. These come in the form of quotes or short paragraphs taken from my notes and experiences. Then there are bonus questions. You won't earn any extra points, but you may find just what you need in them.

Answer the questions. These will help you apply the lessons.

Then you are finished, if you want to be. Use the goal or blank pages as you wish and as the Holy Spirit guides you.

This book can be used by an individual or in a group like our class. If you are doing this study on your own, be sure to tell a friend what you are learning.

Topics for Three Months

Month 1
Surrender/ Attributes of God/Prayer/Grace

Month 2
Bible Study/Goals and Objectives /Key Concepts

Month 3
Mentors and Mentoring/Laughter/Temptation/Friendship

9 More Bonus Pages
Covenant/Imagination/Come/Armor

Homiletics

Mind Mapping

1—This Month is _____

In the Year _____

Goals This Month with Objectives
for Meeting Them

_____

_____

_____

_____

_____

_____

_____

_____

_____

_____

_____

Week 1, Day 1

Date_____

TBtG 1_____

TBtG 2_____

TBtG 3_____

Instruction

This is tough. I have so much to tell you. Where to begin? I'll start with the best word I ever learned-it is not *supercalifragilisticexpialidocious,* –though it is similar in a way. *Surrender.* As you read in my testimony, God used the hymn "I Surrender All" to bring me to himself. Now, having completed dozens of Bible studies, hundreds of lessons, and having heard a bazillion sermons, every spiritual question seems be answered, at least in part, in this word. God wants us to give him all of our concerns and all our joys-as well-as an offering. So when you have heartache, deliver it to him. When you are complimented, deliver that to him. When you find yourself in the lowest valley, on the highest mountain, or somewhere along the way, surrender it back to the one who gave it to you in the first place.

Question

What is God asking you to surrender today?

Week 1, Day 2

Date_____

TBtG 1_____

TBtG 2_____

TBtG 3_____

Instruction

Surrender might be explained best by comparing it to riding a tandem bicycle –you know, the kind with two seats: one in front of the other. Some days we sit up front and steer, and we hit potholes, get splashed, and maybe even fly over the handlebars occasionally. On other days we let Jesus steer, and he takes all the pressure off. We simply pedal.

Question

Who's going to ride up front today?

Week 1, Day 3

Date_____

TBtG 1_____

TBtG 2_____

TBtG 3_____

Fortunately, great songs are still being written. I like the work of Stuart Townend and Kristen and Keith Getty. "In Christ Alone" and "The Power of the Cross" move me almost as much as my initial hymn-filling salvation experience at camp. I tried my hand at writing hymn lyrics by adding a verse to "I Surrender All." It meets my typical daily need and goes like this: "All to Jesus, I surrender, now I pray your peace be mine. Help me see life all-in-perspective, trusting you to make things fine."

Questions

What is your favorite hymn or praise song?

Write your own line to Jesus. How does it go?

Week 2, Day 1

Date_____

TBtG 1_____

TBtG 2_____

TBtG 3_____

Instruction

Deo volente means pretty much the same thing as surrender: "whatever God wants" -with the implication that the person saying it, actually means it. There's surrender again. But it may remind you of a poplar shrug, "whatever," which carries the connotation of apathy. This is not apathy. This is active relinquishment of personal preferences to God's will. I find it very hard to discern sometimes because I love making my own plans. Just as an artist or designer signs his or her work as proof that the work is sufficient or finished, we need to ask God to sign off on our work. It's all really his anyway.

Question

What plans of yours need submitting to God for a signature?

Week 2, Day 2

Date_____

TBtG 1_____

TBtG 2_____

TBtG 3_____

Instruction

During our small adult group study using John Ortberg's *God is Closer than You Think*, we learned another surrender phrase, "As you wish," like what Farm Boy says to Buttercup in the film *The Princess Bride*. "Farm Boy," a.k.a. "Westley," declares his unconditional love for Buttercup every time he says this.

Questions

<u>Circle one of the following</u>: Developing the habit of saying "as you wish, Lord" (a.) sounds way too hard right now, (b.) is possible, (c.) might be possible, or (d.) will work for me.

In any case, how might this action be comparable to Westley's?

Week 2, Day 3

Date_____

TBtG 1_____

TBtG 2_____

TBtG 3_____

Instruction

Megan, Molly, Jenny, and Sarah have seen my Bible. It is like a miniature file cabinet with stuff overflowing. In it (somewhere) is a bookmark from Precept Ministries that has a list of the names of God. These are worth learning as an aid to praising him.

Think about how sweet the sound of your name is to your ears. Imagine how sweet his name sounds to him!

Let's start with this one: *Elohim*. Say it with this phonetic pronunciation: "*ello heeem*" (like "Jell-O bean"). This God name means "Creator."

Question

Think of three things God has created for which you would like to praise him right now.

Week 3, Day 1

Date_____

TBtG 1_____

TBtG 2_____

TBtG 3_____

Instruction

Some other names of God are *Jehovah-jireh*: the Lord will provide; *Jehovah-shalom*: the Lord is Peace; and *Jehovah-tsidkenu*: the Lord our righteousness. I especially like *Jehovah-nissi*- the Lord my banner- because it reminds me that he is a triumphant and a picture-rich God who surely loves pageantry as much as I do.

Question

If you were to design a banner that expresses your love for God, what color would it be and what would it say?

Week 3, Day 2

Date_____

TBtG 1_____

TBtG 2_____

TBtG 3_____

Instruction

Attributes of God include the following things you can ascribe to or simply say about him. He is just. He is faithful. He is forgiving. He is kind. And he is compassionate. These I have before me every day in the form of my license plate: JF4KC.

Look for him. Look for ways to remember him. And don't forget to praise him when you do find him.

Question

Where or in whom do you see a praiseworthy reminder of God?

Week 3, Day 3

Date_____

TBtG 1_____

TBtG 2_____

TBtG 3_____

Instruction

Also at the top of my list is teaching you the ACTS of prayer. This simple acrostic stands for Adoration, Confession, Thanksgiving, and Supplication. You already have the fourth part licked. Asking for stuff is easy.

(Personal note: I vividly remember my dad teaching me these. I treasure the scrap of paper on which he wrote them for me.)

Question

What do you need to confess? You've already thanked him. Now tell him what you need. You can even ask for things you *want* if you think they may be in line with his will.

Week 4, Day 1

Date_____

TBtG 1_____

TBtG 2_____

TBtG 3_____

Instruction

In addition to praying for yourself, I know you'll want to pray for your friends or for your children. To pray effectively for your children, you need to know them. You do that by studying how they are bent-the direction God has given them to go. Read more about this in Dr. Joe Temple's book, *Know Your Child,* and Dr. Chuck Swindoll's *You and Your Child.* But first read this verse.

Proverbs 22:6: "Start children off on the way they should go, and even when they are old they will not turn from it."

Question

How might really knowing your friends help you pray for them?

Week 4, Day 2

Date_____

TBtG 1_____

TBtG 2_____

TBtG 3_____

Instruction

Grace. It can mean so many things like elegance, favor, good will or even moral strength. In the Bible it often means "unmerited favor" as in Ephesians 2:5 and Titus 3:5. It is saving and justifying grace. It can also mean attractiveness, as in Colossians 4:6: "Let your conversation be always full of grace, seasoned with salt, so that you may know how to answer everyone."

Questions

Circle one of the following: What is grace? (a.) A prayer at dinner. (b.) A beautiful name. (c.) A famous movie star. (d.) When you aren't a klutz.

How have you been shown grace as "unmerited favor?"

How have you shared grace in your relationships?

Week 4, Day 3

Date_____

TBtG 1_____

TBtG 2_____

TBtG 3_____

Instruction

Grace is one of the five solos, or Latin phrases that summarize the tenets of the Protestant Reformation. They are *sola scriptura*, by scripture alone, *sola fide*, by faith alone; *sola gratia*, by grace alone; *solo Christo*, by Christ alone; and *solo Deo gloria*, glory to God alone. These radical sixteenth-century ideas set off a firestorm that remains controversial today. Consider your position on these statements.

Questions

What are the foundations for your faith? What or who saves or has saved you? How? And to what purpose or to whose advantage do you live, work, and play?

Week 4 Bonus

Date_____

TBtG 1_____

TBtG 2_____

TBtG 3_____

Instruction

The Golden Rule is found in Christianity, Confucianism, Hinduism, Islam, Jainism, Buddhism, Baha'i, Native American Indian and Ancient Egyptian worship. (There are more on the list, too.) In the Bible you can find it in Leviticus 19:18 and 34, Matthew 7:12, and Luke 6:27-36. In Leviticus we are charged with loving others as ourselves. The Matthew passage says that it sums up the Law and the Prophets. I sum it up with two words: be kind. It is the only rule in my classroom, because when it is followed, even those who do not merit favor receive it-and there is productivity.

Questions

What do grace and the Golden Rule have in common?

Why do think this concept appears to be universal?

Note: Stay tuned for more about grace.

2—This Month Is_____

In the Year _____

Goals This Month with Objectives
for Meeting Them

_____

_____

_____

_____

_____

_____

_____

_____

_____

_____

_____

_____

Week 1, Day 1

Date_____

TBtG 1_____

TBtG 2_____

TBtG 3_____

Instruction

I like to use Kay Arthur's method for marking my study Bible, and I recommend it to you here. Select colors for things like love, peace, praying, eternal truths, attributes of God, surrender verses—whatever you like to track most. Circle or underline words or phrases according to color. In addition, code passages with simple symbols. I code saving and sanctifying grace with a brown cross. God gets a triangle since he's at the top of a triangular relationship with Jesus and me. Christ gets a blue line attached to a cross. The Holy Spirit is the cloud always hovering nearby. Gifts I mark with a box and a bow. The result is that when you look at a passage, the repeated words and key concepts will leap off the page.

The apostle Paul used the word—grace—over one hundred times. In your study Bible, find a dozen of those uses. Mark them however you like.

Question

What can you learn from this and other marking exercises?

Week 1, Day 2

Date_____

TBtG 1_____

TBtG 2_____

TBtG 3_____

Instruction

Kay Arthur's *Lord, I Need Grace to Make It* Bible study impacted me a lot partly because, somewhere along my journey through it, God challenged me to list all the points of grace I could find. I came up with 61, and those sixty-one rays of light still make my heart soar. If you ever need *anything*, you can bet that there is grace for it. Read 2 Corinthians 12:9 and 10.

Question

Where might God's grace be waiting to meet your weakness?

Week 1, Day 3

Date_____

TBtG 1_____

TBtG 2_____

TBtG 3_____

Instruction

While I've set aside three pages for goal-setting with objectives for reaching them at the beginning of each section, I've left you without suggestions for that part of the diary until now. Perhaps you have found your own way. Perhaps you are glad to have some guidance now.

Think of the goals as the end of a journey, and the objectives are the legs of the trip. What roads do I need to take to get me to_____?

Example: My goal is to become a doctor. My objectives include passing biology and chemistry, and then shadowing a local pediatrician.

Your assignment is to pray for God to open your mind to his plan for your life. Take a pencil and paper as you pray so you can jot down what you learn.

Question

What did God reveal?

Week 2, Day 1

Date_____

TBtG 1_____

TBtG 2_____

TBtG 3_____

Instruction

The danger of a life driven by goals is running ahead of God and accepting unnecessary burdens on our time. I've read two books about setting proper limits, *Margin* by Richard Swenson, and *Boundaries* by Henry Cloud and John Townsend. I recommend both books to those of you with tendencies to overdo.

Question

Are you an over-achiever? If so, pray twice about the goals and objectives you write down. Make sure they are in keeping with God's will and purpose for you by measuring them against the strength he provides and the peace you experience. Trim activities and commitments as much as you can until you experience peace.

Week 2, Day 2

Date_____

TBtG 1_____

TBtG 2_____

TBtG 3_____

Instruction

In Dr. Swenson's book I particularly like this: "Time urgency in Christ's lifestyle is conspicuously absent...overloaded schedules are not the way to walk in His steps." Christ was never hurried. (NavPress, page 169)

That may not seem possible in our fast-paced competitive world. But it can be an important safeguard for our goal-setting.

Question

What goals and objectives might you revise now?

Week 2, Day 3

Date_____

TBtG 1_____

TBtG 2_____

TBtG 3_____

Instruction

What do you know about your gifts, strengths and weaknesses? Do you know your spiritual gifts? Make a list of your known intellectual, spiritual, creative, and social gifts and skills. Make another list of your weaknesses.

If you have never taken spiritual gifts assessment, take one online or ask your pastor (or Sunday school teacher) to administer one. Read these verses to get a head start: 1 Corinthians 12, Romans 12:4-8 and 1 Peter 4:11.

Question

What did you discover? Summarize that here.

Week 3, Day 1

Date_____

TBtG 1_____

TBtG 2_____

TBtG 3_____

Instruction

For more self-discovery, look up the Myers-Briggs personality test. Knowing your personality type and how you fit in the body of Christ can help you pare down your goals. As always, the key to knowing is to pray for illumination by the Holy Spirit.

Question

Are you sensing that you are "on track" with your plans? If not, take a break to renew your energies by going on a walk or scheduling a short vacation. I find that taking time away from my typical schedule often fixes a confused state of mind.

Week 3, Day 2

Date_____

TBtG 1_____

TBtG 2_____

TBtG 3_____

Instruction

Among the most important biblical concepts are certainly *The Ten Commandments*. In summary, they're really pretty simple. First, worship God alone. Second, don't make any idols. Third, don't curse using God's name. Fourth and fifth: don't forget to rest or to call your mom and dad. Sixth and seventh: don't kill anyone or commit adultery. Finally: don't steal, lie, or think for a moment that you entitled to something that belongs to someone else. (Yes, this is my paraphrase.)

Ephesians 6:1-3 comments on the fifth one: "Children, obey your parents in the Lord, for this is right. 'Honor your father and mother' –which is the first commandment with a promise– 'so that it may go well with you and that you may enjoy long life on the earth.'"

Questions

How might things go well for us if we obey this commandment?

Why is honoring our parents so important?

Week 3, Day 3

Date_____

TBtG 1_____

TBtG 2_____

TBtG 3_____

Instruction

Underscoring everything biblical is a respect for life itself. It is one of three cornerstone values: respect for life, marriage and property. Here's what Mother Teresa had to say about this ongoing debate.

"In February 1997 at the National Prayer Breakfast in Washington attended by the President and the First Lady: 'What is taking place in America,' she said, 'is a war against the child. And if we accept that the mother can kill her own child, how can we tell other people not to kill one another.' She also said: 'Any country that accepts abortion, is not teaching its people to love, but to use any violence to get what it wants.'"

Questions

Have you made up your mind? Is abortion a liberty we should not deny any woman? More importantly, what do you believe God thinks? If you need help deciding, read Psalm 139.

Week 4, Day 1

Date_____

TBtG 1_____

TBtG 2_____

TBtG 3_____

Instruction

Work is a privilege. That's why I love Ecclesiastes. My college friend, Joy Huffman, read the entire book aloud while I drove us from Houston to Lubbock. When she stopped reading, when the book ended, I recall the feeling of letdown…disappointment that this amazing series of lessons ended when it did. The beauty of the writing felt like warm laundry in my arms.

The author's attitude toward work teaches balance in life, like in this great passage: "Moreover, when God gives any man wealth and possessions, and enables him to enjoy them, to accept his lot and be happy in his work–this is a gift of God." Ecclesiastes 5:19

Questions

Circle one of the following: For me, work or school is (a.) drudgery, (b.) almost always challenging, (c.) a mixture of good and bad experiences, (d.) a real joy.

What can you do to see your work as a gift from God?

Week 4, Day 2

Date_____

TBtG 1_____

TBtG 2_____

TBtG 3_____

Instruction

Ecclesiastes celebrates the provision of fellowship, too.

Ecclesiastes 4:9-12 says, "Two are better than one, because they have a good return for their work: If one falls down, his friend can help him up. But pity the man who falls and has no one to help him up! Also, if two lie down together, they will keep warm. But how can one keep warm alone? Though one may be overpowered, two can defend themselves. A cord of three strands is not quickly broken."

Question

What or who is the third cord or strand?

Why is a three-cord relationship best?

Week 4, Day 3

Date_____

TBtG 1_____

TBtG 2_____

TBtG 3_____

Instruction

Restoration. I love that word.

One day it finally occurred to me that the theme of the Bible is simply that. And redemption. But I understand restoration more concretely than redemption since human beings can restore a building, restore a pantry, or restore a relationship. Redemption is a mystery that only God can engineer.

God created this marvelous world. He added mankind to take care of it and for his own pleasure. Often the created ones forget who made everything that they enjoy-possible. The reports recorded in the Bible reveal a series of noble efforts and infamous mistakes. We can become more qualified builders, restorers, and day laborers if we study their stories in the guidebook.

Questions

What restoration or redemption story first pops into mind?

If you need to look for one, where will you look first, and why?

3—This Month Is_____

In the Year _____

Goals This Month with Objectives
for Meeting Them

_____

_____

_____

_____

_____

_____

_____

_____

_____

_____

_____

Week 1, Day 1

Date_____

TBtG 1_____

TBtG 2_____

TBtG 3_____

Instruction

We have explored five key biblical concepts: *The Ten Commandments*, the privilege of work, fellowship, and restoration.

This week we'll begin to look at notable things to learn from the Bible: from wise women and mentors, to wise and trusted people who have guided us.

Questions

Who is your favorite wise woman from the Bible?

Why?

Who is your favorite hometown wise woman?

Why?

Week 1, Day 2

Date_____

TBtG 1_____

TBtG 2_____

TBtG 3_____

Instruction and Questions

What wisdom did you receive from your mom or a motherly mentor? How did she set the example of a wise woman?

Read Proverbs 31 and fill in the following blanks.

1. My mother/mentor brought good, not harm all the days of her life by_____
_____.

2. My mother/mentor set about her work_____
_____.

3. My mother/mentor opened her arms to others by _____
_____
_____.

4. My mother/mentor showed that she carried a light heart by _____
_____.

5. My mother/mentor faithfully instructed me _____
_____
_____.

6. My mother/mentor watched over the affairs of her household by _____
_____.

Week 1, Day 3

Date_____

TBtG 1_____

TBtG 2_____

TBtG 3_____

Instruction

Read Proverbs 31 again. The last point is particularly significant because women need to be adored, praised, and encouraged to fully carry out their tasks *in* the home and *out* of it.

Questions

Was your mother or mentor praised at home? If so, by whom, and what effect did it have on her?

If your answer is no, what effect did this have on you?

Week 2, Day 1

Date_____

TBtG 1_____

TBtG 2_____

TBtG 3_____

Instruction

Ephesians 4:29 says, "Do not let any unwholesome talk come out of your mouths, but only what is helpful for building others up according to their needs, that it may benefit those who listen."

It is equally true that women should work to build up others in the home as well as beyond its walls.

Question

Even if we have not seen positive modeling of this behavior, we are obligated to guard our words and to encourage one another. How might one who has not had adequate encouragement still learn to become an encourager?

Week 2, Day 2

Date_____

TBtG 1_____

TBtG 2_____

TBtG 3_____

Instruction

"Laughter is carbonated holiness." – Anne Lamott

I might not agree with Anne on all points, but this is too cute and it seems all too true to leave out of this study. It also gets me to my next few questions.

Questions

Could laughter really be part of the Christian journey? If that is true, why is it? If not, why not?

Who makes you laugh? Why?

Have you laughed today?

Week 2, Day 3

Date_____

TBtG 1_____

TBtG 2_____

TBtG 3_____

Instruction

An edition of *Parade Magazine* featured *The Parade Family Health Quiz: How health-savvy are you? Take our test to find out.* Emily Listfield, *Parade Magazine*, January 9, 2011, page 16.

One of the items on the quiz tests one's knowledge of ways to practice self-control. "To help you pass up that second piece of chocolate cake, you should: (a.) Vow to get on the scale the next morning. (b.) Remind yourself that it won't look good on your hips. (c.) Make a fist. (d.) Keep a bag of carrots and other healthy snacks hand. The answer is (c.) For an instant hit of will power, clench your fist. A new study published in the Journal of Consumer Research (the article continues) found that tightening your muscles when faced with temptation can help shore up your self-control. One caveat: It only works in the moment–meaning, while you're actually staring down that slice." I see a spiritual application. Just as resisting another chocolate truffle is hard, so it is with other issues, like those bad thoughts that continually cycle through our brains as worries or hurts. Read II Corinthians 10:5 to see this amazing truth. Activate the scripture by clenching your fist as you take captive a bad thought and make it obedient to Christ.

Question Did it work?

Week 3, Day 1

Date_____

TBtG 1_____

TBtG 2_____

TBtG 3_____

Instruction

The words "faithful are the wounds of a friend" (from the King James Version of a Proverbs 27:6) came to mind after reading a note from my pal, Kathy Strong.

I was suffering through a tough patch, and she saw the flaws in my reasoning. Having known each other from childhood–actually, the cradle roll at church, and now, having known each other deeply over the past couple of decades, she also sensed the root of my flawed thinking. What she shared at the peak of my little crisis was pure love. It hurt a bit, but it caused me to turn the corner in my battle. Other close buddies have done the same thing. Much of what I have to say about friendship should be credited to them. For you Jane Austen fans, consider the example of Mr. Knightly in *Emma*.

Questions

Look up Proverbs 27:5-6 and 9. Would you rather experience open rebuke or hidden love? Have you ever received helpful wounds or earnest counsel from a friend? Can you also give it? How are rebukes different from insults? Use a blank page if you need it.

Week 3, Day 2

Date_____

TBtG 1_____

TBtG 2_____

TBtG 3_____

Instruction

Growing up in the sixties in a small West Texas city in a new housing area, there were always lots of kids and lots of undeveloped spaces to explore. After chores were completed, the kids in my neighborhood had the freedom to spend what remained of the day outside if we liked. No sunscreen. No worries that someone would take us—except maybe when the Fair was in town. This freedom created the opportunity for developing friendships. I still treasure them and the memories we made together, but the closest tie has always been with a girl I met at church: Melinda Ann Stone, now, Mrs. Gordon.

Melinda and I attended different elementary schools, but met up in Junior High and High School. We were in each other's weddings, and we now write or call each other every week. I count her as one of the sweetest gifts of life.

Question

What or who are your sweetest gifts so far?

Week 3, Day 3

Date_____

TBtG 1_____

TBtG 2_____

TBtG 3_____

Instruction

As you are well aware, not all relationships are like Melinda's and mine. Girls–and women–can be mean. I experienced this first-hand in elementary school, and the scars run deep. But as Romans 8:28 teaches, they came with purpose. I am grateful for the scars that have taught me to show compassion.

Questions

Could you qualify as a "mean girl?" If so, how have you been "mean?" And what does it mean to be "mean?"

Is bullying a problem in your school or neighborhood? If so, what could you do to help stop it?

Week 4, Day 1

Date_____

TBtG 1_____

TBtG 2_____

TBtG 3_____

Instruction

I caught an interview with a bully on television recently. It revealed that bullies (and this was a girl) enjoy bullying because it gives them a sense of power over others. We also know that bullies tend to find easy targets.

Questions

What can you do to avoid becoming the victim of a bully? What spiritual lessons are there to be learned from these behaviors-for both the bully and the bullied?

Week 4, Day 2

Date_____

TBtG 1_____

TBtG 2_____

TBtG 3_____

Instruction

Hebrews 12:15 says "See to it that no one misses the grace of God and that that no bitter root grows up to cause trouble and defile many." Sometimes we are simply insulted, or in another word: wronged. It is not always possible to live in peace with all men. But we should never become bitter—either way. I have learned something that helps me understand how these wrongs occur, and how we can avoid the bitter root that often develops with them.

Hurt occurs when someone insults our self-image or how see ourselves.

Our best friends are those who mirror a perception of us that is positive. If we perceive superiority through a condescending remark or failure to reciprocate, unfair judgment, or outright distrust, the friendship will be in jeopardy. When this happens, ask God to repair it. If he chooses not to, and you know that you are fully cooperating with him, move on.

Question

I have a tendency to bury, and then retrieve, old wounds. This then leads to bitterness. I hope you don't do this, but if you do, how might you see to it that no bitter root causes trouble and defiles you?

Week 4, Day 3

Date_____

TBtG 1_____

TBtG 2_____

TBtG 3_____

Instruction

In a nod to other friendships that have brought me wisdom and joy, those that have been like Jonathan to David, I close this section on friendship with helpful quotes from friends.

"We each need different tools to bring us to the foot of the cross." Hollye Jaklewicz

"God is too scary without Jesus between us and God." Mary Gregory

"The best friends are those we consider safe spots." Mendy Phelps

Ruth's Way: "1. Take care of yourself. Eat, sleep and exercise. 2. Stay busy. 3. Share with those in need." Ruth Jackson

Question

Will you choose to be that friend who encourages and sharpens?

Bonus 2

TBtG 1_____

TBtG 2_____

TBtG 3_____

Instruction

Covenant. In Hebrew: *beryth* = a compact; Greek: *diatheke* = a contract. The word "made" in Hebrew, *karath*, means to cut, so the making of a compact meant literally "to cut a covenant."

The Bible tells us in Genesis 15:9-11 and 17-21 that the covenant with Abram was attested to with the shedding of blood. Blood represents a covering for sin in the Old Testament, whereas it is symbolic of cleansing in the New Testament. Most OT covenants featured a blood sacrifice, a meal, promises, signs, and the exchange of gifts. The covenant parties cut the sacrifice and then walked in a figure eight through pieces. They did this to signify their death to self and the fact that they wanted God to cut them in half like the sacrifice if they broke the covenant. The book *The Miracle of the Scarlet Thread* by Richard Booker explains the steps of Old Testament covenant-making. (Destiny Image Publishers, Shippensburg, PA, 1981.)

Questions

Who initiated the New Covenant of grace?

What is the basis of this covenant? Why should you care?

Bonus 3

Date_____

TBtG 1_____

TBtG 2_____

TBtG 3_____

Instruction

The most important covenant is the one found in the New Testament. Only the first three gospels: Matthew, Mark, and Luke mention it by name, and only in reference to the Eucharist or the Lord's Supper. But the New Testament books lay out the form for living under this new contract with God-with Christ as mediator. Read Hebrews 9:15.

Question

What are God's gifts or blessings when a person has entered into covenant with Jesus Christ? You may refer to the whole contract (any part of the New Testament) for your answer.

Bonus 4

Date_____

TBtG 1_____

TBtG 2_____

TBtG 3_____

Instruction

The customary way to ratify a contract in the time of the Old Testament was to follow the instructions put forth in Genesis 15. Today we sign documents, or at the very least we make a promise with a handshake. In courtrooms and on Inauguration Day, we even see people make oaths with an upraised right hand and with the left hand on a Bible.

Questions

What experience have you had in making covenants? Have you signed a lease, borrowed money, or promised a friend to never ever tell her secrets? How seriously do you take these commitments?

Bonus 5

Date_____

TBtG 1_____

TBtG 2_____

TBtG 3_____

Instruction

There are eight covenants in the Bible—eight divine ordinances with signs or pledges. The number eight stands for superabundance. It can mean beyond completeness—which is signified by the number seven. There are also eight beatitudes or blessings.

See E.W. Bullinger's *Numbers in Scripture: Its Supernatural Design and Spiritual Significance.* (Grand Rapids, MI: Kregel Publications, 1967)

Questions

In light of your knowledge about the number eight, what do eight contracts and eight blessings tell us about the nature of God and his relationship to us?

Bonus 6

Date_____

TBtG 1_____

TBtG 2_____

TBtG 3_____

Instruction

Imagine. I love this word.

My sister, Jane, gave me a metal sign with this word. It hangs in my studio. Every morning and lots of times during the day I am reminded to let my brain expand a bit; to explore possibilities. Even if this word were not referenced in my study Bible concordance, I would know Jesus values the imagination because of the stories he painted in his sermons. Ephesians 3:20-21 offers strong evidence that God knows our capacity to think outside the box. "Now to him who is able to do immeasurably more than all we ask or imagine, according to his power that is at work within us, to him be glory in the church and in Christ Jesus throughout all generations, forever and ever! Amen." This benediction both praises God and encourages us to ask him for things beyond our imaginations. Wow.

Question

What will you imagine he wants you to know or do today?

Bonus 7

Date_____

TBtG 1_____

TBtG 2_____

TBtG 3_____

Instruction

Come. It's the first word of Matthew 11.

Our response to that word is much like the command to surrender. It carries a condition. If we come to Christ, we receive rest. If we take his yoke–if we agree to get in step and learn from him, the one who is gentle and humble in heart–THEN we will have rest for our souls.

Hanging out with Christ brings us back to the moment we surrendered to him the first time. It is again well with our souls. We are restored.

Questions

In the Psalms we see the word *"selah"*. It means to measure and reflect. How might you come to Christ to measure and reflect? What would you do?

Bonus 8

Date_____

TBtG 1_____

TBtG 2_____

TBtG 3_____

Instruction

"Come" also reminds me of the word "abide," the topic of John 15. After we come to Christ, and after we measure and reflect, it is best to abide–remain, or stay connected. Read John 15 to get the full story about how you have been grafted into God's family tree.

Question

What are the benefits of abiding or remaining in him?

Bonus 9

Date_____

TBtG 1_____

TBtG 2_____

TBtG 3_____

Instruction

Wear armor.

"Unguarded strength is double weakness because that is where the 'retired sphere of the leasts' saps. The Bible characters fell on their strong points, never on their weak ones." Oswald Chambers, *My Utmost for His Highest*, April 19.

Ephesians 6:10-18 outlines the "full armor of God." There are six pieces of gear we can put on—with prayer and alertness being the operative mode for a soldier of Christ. This armor helps us protect our weaknesses and shore up our strengths so that we do not fall on our strong points.

The belt of truth defends against lies. The breastplate of righteousness can be used to against attacks against emotions. Gospel shoes make you ready to share your faith with a friend. The shield of faith defends against the arrows of insults, setbacks and temptations. The helmet of salvation protects your mind from doubting God's saving work the sword of the Spirit—the only offensive weapon—helps you trust in the truth of God's word. *-Life Application Bible*

Questions: Which of these pieces of armor do you need most today? Why?

Bonus 10

Date_____

TBtG 1_____

TBtG 2_____

TBtG 3_____

Instruction

This final bonus is simply my prayer for you, taken from a passage that my oldest friend, Melinda, and I pray for our children.

As part of Paul's opening prayer in Colossians 1, I've titled it "Finding Purpose and Meaning in Following Christ Jesus."

9 For this reason, since the day we heard about you, we have not stopped praying for you and asking God to fill you with the knowledge of his will through all spiritual wisdom and understanding. 10 And we pray this in order that you may live a life worthy of the Lord and may please him in every way: bearing fruit in every good work, growing in the knowledge of God, 11 being strengthened with all power according to his glorious might so that you may have great endurance and patience, and joyfully 12 giving thanks to the Father, who has qualified you to share in the inheritance of the saints in the kingdom of light. 13 For he has rescued us from the dominion of darkness and brought us into the kingdom of the Son he loves, 14 in whom we have redemption, the forgiveness of sins.

Questions: What is your favorite phrase in this passage? Why?

Homiletics

As part of my training to become a Bible Study Fellowship (BSF) Substitute Teaching Leader, I had to learn the art of homiletics. I call it an art, for it fits the definition: any skill or mastery. And the exercise does inspire creativity. Some of my greatest moments of divine inspiration have come while dissecting a passage of Scripture using this simple method of biblical analysis. Most people who learn this skill become teachers, but it is certainly equally useful in personal study. I find it thrilling.

Here are the steps as outlined by the 1983 BSF *Discussion Leaders' Manual*. I've shortened some of the instructions where we'll not lose clarity.

Step I: Read the passage thoroughly.

1. Choose a book, a chapter or just a few verses.
2. Make a list of the events, topics or conversations in the passage. I learned to refer to them as "themes, scenes, and events." This should be a list of five to twenty items. Ask yourself: "What is this about?"
3. Look for repeated words or phrases which seem to characterize the whole passage. Write those or underline them in your Bible.

Step II: Group the items into paragraphs.

1. Bracket the items into paragraphs.
2. Using these paragraphs, divide the passage into its main divisions. Use a sentence as a heading to describe each division.
3. Make a note of the verses pertaining to each paragraph.

Step III: Create a Subject Sentence of not more than ten words.
This summative sentence must have a subject and a verb.

Step IV: Ask yourself: "What is the aim of this passage? What should the audience do now?" List this as Cause the Audience To: or CAT:

Step V: Apply it by asking three to five key questions.

As the instructions note: strive for clarity, brevity and simplicity. Our example for that is, of course, Christ.

One Example

Passage - John 15:1-17

I: Themes, Scenes and Events

1-2 Jesus (the son) is the vine and his Father is the gardener who prunes branches.

3 The word cleanses.

4-5 Branches (we) must stay in the vine (Jesus) to bear fruit.

6-7 Branches that don't retain the vine's words don't remain (get burned up).

8 God is glorified by fruitful disciples.

9-10 Obey commands us to remain in his love and have joy.

12-13 Love as he loved us, sacrificially.

14-15 Jesus' friends do as he commands, equal in knowledge.

16a We were chosen and appointed to bear lasting fruit.

16b Fruit bearers are given what is asked in Jesus' name.

17 We must love one another.

II: Passage Divisions

(Verses 1-8) I. Branches must remain in the vine to bear fruit.

(Verses 9-17) II. Branches must remain in the vine's love as friends.

III: Passage Summary (a Ten-Word Sentence)

Branches must remain in the vine and in Jesus' love.

IV. Passage Aim–What should result from this study/what it should "cause the audience to do"?

CAT: Retain Jesus' commands and remain in fellowship with Him

V. Passage Application Questions (Be sure to answer these.)

(Verse 2) 1. Are you a branch undergoing pruning? If so, in what ways?

(Verse 3) 2. How has the word made you clean?

(Verses 4-5) 3. When have you tried fruit-bearing on your own? What were the results? Has remaining or abiding become a habit? If so, how?

(Verse13) 4. How have you given your life sacrificially?

(Verses 14-15) 5. How do you feel about your position as a friend to Jesus?

(Verse 16) 6. When you ask in Jesus' name, what are you ultimately doing?

Mind Mapping

I've included this activity because it is a helpful tool for sorting out your life or a difficult subject like "Post-Modernism." Sarah and Megan know it well from their art history course with me. And if you are a fan of the website FastCompany, you know how cool these can be. The FastCompany people call them "infographics." But they have a long history. "Mr. Renaissance," Leonardo da Vinci, made them. And I learned them as "bubble diagrams" at Texas Tech University in the late 1970s. Professor and architect, Alex Karther, taught us to create floor plans using this method. It has been a gift for me–a person with what seems like scrambled eggs on the brain some days. Here's how you do it.

First–get out your favorite pencils or marker and write your main objective in the middle of the paper.

Second–if there are equivalent ideas or concepts, put those in the middle, too. Draw color-coded boxes or circles around them. The object is to begin seeing connections.

Third–write connecting, dependent, correlating ideas near the objectives that relate.

Finally–draw arrows, bullet lists, and/or draw symbols to illustrate your concepts and see relationships.

Here's one based on this book:

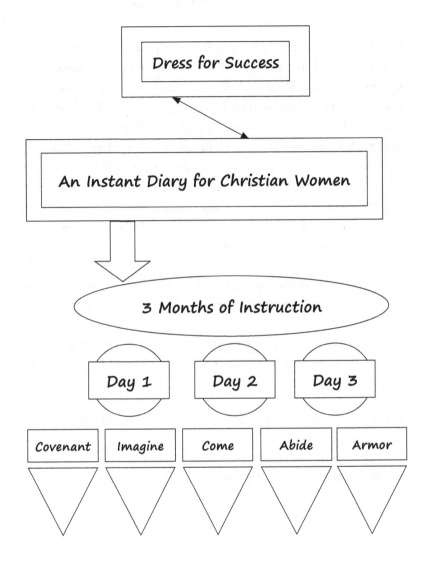

Final Words

What you've been reading is actually an improved version of the original book I shared with Megan, Molly, Jenny, and Sarah. I've taken some time to finally smooth out some of the phrasing and correct a lot of mistakes, as well as add some clarifying content. While it is still imperfect, I hope it will bless you or someone you know.

Since life is always a journey with a purpose, here are a couple of things I've been learning since I first put this together for my class.

First: We can look for God to fill our buckets every day, and we will be amazed at what he supplies. Just like the Israelites in the wilderness, God will provide manna (literally, "what is it"). Our manna-our daily provisions- cannot be stored up, reconstituted, or duplicated. I found that with a husband and son half a world away a few summers ago, a daughter alone on the East Coast, a daughter-in-law yet to meet, a new job starting in two months, and bad news just in on the medical front for my dad, God is still in control. He gave me fresh energy, fresh vision and refreshing activities with others.

Second: We can love someone we've yet to meet. When I updated this book, my daughter-in-law was brand new to our family, and we'd only met via Skype and email. Yet I adored her already. Now, several years later, I can add a hearty "amen" to that!

Keep looking to Him through scriptures, songs, fellowship and of course, prayer.

In His grace,

Marianne

Notes

Notes

Notes

Notes

Notes

Notes

Notes

Notes

Notes

Notes

Notes

Notes

Notes

Notes

_____

_____

_____

_____

_____

_____

_____

_____

_____

_____

_____

_____

_____

_____

Notes

_____

_____

_____

_____

_____

_____

_____

_____

_____

_____

_____

_____

_____

_____

Notes

Notes

Notes

Notes

_____

_____

_____

_____

_____

_____

_____

_____

_____

_____

_____

_____

_____

_____

_____

_____

Printed in the United States
By Bookmasters